TIGER

A book of poetry by

Tim Pangburn

*Written during the summer of 2021,
in a furious fever dream.*

*This book is dedicated to the muse,
without whom the artist could not create.*

Clever Girl

Communication has broken down and all that is left is silence and staring eyes. With one hand, I can shatter a captive gaze. With one word, I can force these actions. End this. Just finish me and end this. Gnashing teeth and streaks of scarlet paint the evening a shade of red familiar yet so far away.

Sacrificial Trinkets

Time is in decay, and my heart along with it. Distance has broken my hope and all that remains is despair at what could have been. I am yours to wear like the skin of an angel. I am yours to baptize in the blood of the lamb. Stand and fall open like so many music boxes, sounds of beauty rising to a terrible cacophony.

Flagged From the Nitrous

I don't have any words. The screams came in silence, and knocked the wind out of me. My throat clenched for hours, stammering nonsense and partial sentences. I can feel my awkward, drawn out voice. Stretching words. Reaching for a sense of clarity. But nothing comes, and I'm left with lips still wishing to meet yours.

You Only Live Three Times

My rib cage has been hollowed,
and my heart removed, in its place
a black bird. A stare like winter. The
bristling of hairs on your neck. I
have died before, but never like
this.

A Slow Paced Cello

I watch the sky go dark and run my fingers through my hair. Here I stand, on the precipice of glory and insanity, and all I can do is fall. Fall to the ground, fall to my knees, it doesn't matter which. Or falling through space and time because neither exist in your presence. I am a child again, and I am old and withered. I am shaking off the ash of 1,000 burning cities that ignited at the sound of your voice. The greatest tragedies are always played in symphonies.

Fire on Golgotha

Defiled like a burning church.
Bludgeoned to death in an alley. In
this place, the only tears shed are
for our suffering, and the only
sympathy we feel is self pity. The
arched windows of a temple,
blacked out in the eclipse,
shattered by the first stone.

A Vulture's Opus

Everything you've ever said was wiped away in one moment. Insecurities are bastards who point fingers and cast blame, and they love me with the whole of their wretched little hearts. Just carry me home and tell me everything's going to be alright, even as you pick the meat from my bones.

Gaia's Loom

When this is over, nothing will be
the same. Unraveled like a spindle
of thread. As cold as the winter
that has settled in my soul. Wipe
tears from my face, but only to
save face. The astronaut cut free,
and floating through space. The
void will swallow me. Earth's barren
womb giving life one more time,
only to smash it into oblivion.

Relapse

Pitch black night, shadowed figures. Scorched earth and mortar fire. We've fought our battles and fled the frontline, but we're beckoned back again. Watch for the light on the horizon. It's not Valhalla, but a path to redemption. You don't need to die in battle, every warrior has earned their seat at the table.

Like Vesuvius, but with iPhones

There are oceans between you and I. Grains of sand like the stars in the sky. When this is over, there will be nuclear shadows. There will be smoke in the crater. The earth will wash over us and preserve us in its clay.

Elephant Memory

Distance makes the heart spoil. Not because it forgets, but because it remembers. It remembers the walls that separate us and the distance between. It remembers your hand in mine, locked in a death grasp for all eternity. A heartbeat turned Morse code, begging you to swallow me into your belly so that I may be born again.

End Times Choreography

Silence is torment, even as the sound of pouring rain deafens me. Thunder breaks the sky. The endless waltz of paranoid delusions dancing in my mind. We pass in twilight, where the sun casts its fire across distant horizons, but the darkness has not yet opened its mouth to devour the children in the night.

Matchsticks

A requiem for daylight, as I will never see it again. I have taken my eyes, for they don't deserve to gaze on such beauty. A crooked smile of bloodied teeth, phantom weeping from dead sockets. The sleight of hand that allows me to feign patience. Take my hand and guide me through the blackened trees, which have withstood tests of fire. I will withstand greater to be blessed with your touch.

Poltergeist Laser

Your presence bore through me like a white hot light. Cauterized, baptized, the Holy Ghost in the shape of a woman. I have felt the hand of god. It was delicate, and promised peace where none existed. It delivered me into your arms.

Mineshaft Canary

As sure as the sun rising in the east, my heart will beat for you, forevermore. There's so much to be said, and I can't think clearly to put it in a straight line. The way crystal beams of light dance in your eyes; the way darkness shines out from behind. With one hand on my throat and the other on my spine, I stand immobilized; your captive bird in cage.

Golem

Lips bleeding the color of crushed berries, using words as brushstrokes to map the landscape of my soul. I'm a heartless automaton, stalking points of light like a hunter follows prey. Self preservation under the cover of night. Skin stretched paper thin and spilling candy hearts from tiny holes.

Astral Projection

Once more through the hourglass,
flesh of my flesh. One more day
our fingers dangle and never touch;
our gaze separated by miles.
Vivisection to locate the soul.
Where reality dies and a eulogy is
delivered through the metaphor of
dreams.

Snake and the Spider

A voice whispers in the dead of night, calling me to abandon sleep. She walks in a gown of gossamer, haunting empty streets. My queen of decay. Serpentine mistress of the highest order. Her veins pump fire and rend flesh from bone. Stripped to my core, I will serve her as her master.

My Own Personal Vietnam

There's a a blackout in communications. Relaying messages by hand. The snipers in their watchtowers, only making headshots. Stick to the shadows. Run. Fucking run. We weave through tall grasses and knotted trees, the only survivors of the massacre. It's all for her.

Truancy

Her voice pushes her words past her lips. "Be with me." The heart pumps the blood. The blood is the life. We walk streets in anonymity, like children dodging curfew. Far ahead of the sirens, and only steps away from the edge of the world.

Tiger

If you look carefully between the vines and elephant ear, you'll see a tiger, prowling for fresh meat. Don't meet its gaze. Don't look its way. It's not the tiger you need worry about, it's me.

Purgatory

Another morning waking without you is another morning in purgatory. I am skin stretched over bone, and bone snapped into place. Traversing oceans of death eternal. The mouths of the sea open and swallow, pushing me into depths of darkness unknown.

<u>Believing the False Reflection</u>

Polished to a mirror finish so I can see just how undeserving I am. Naked and exposed. The words we say are never veiled, and faults will never fracture. Pluck the feathers from the wings. Realign the halo. You are earthbound, yet maintain the perfection of immortals.

Tonight, Sleep Eludes Me

Beyond the shadowed veil of night, our souls entwine. The distance has shattered my will to continue. Somewhere, she drifts to sleep, but I am left restless, clawing at my throat in desperation. Take me, for I am yours, a man bowing unto your perfection.

Dogfight Champ

One gentle touch destroyed everything I am. Now I'm falling at terminal velocity and entering a suicide spiral. Stop me before I hit the ground. Step in and press your lips to mine, and assure me that the world no longer exists.

Headlights to the Ocean

Tonight I drive unlit roads and shed tears at songs I didn't write. We press hand to hand, but the distance is an ocean's reach. So give me to the sea. The guile of serpents. The ritual dance in the garden, beneath falling stars. Give me to the sea and let the currents deliver me to you.

Pale Substitute

I stood naked in the rain, and every drop sent a chill through me. I did it to mimic your touch, because the days we're apart I forget if I'm alive.

Picasso Empowerment

Paint a picture embedded with the deaths of everyone who claimed you. Of every unspoken master. Every high heeled mistress. Let them fall from cliffs and buildings. Let them shatter on the rocks. Paint this picture and reclaim what is yours. Allow the carrion birds to feed.

The Arsonist

I would burn down this city for you.
If it would assuage your worry and
ease your mind, I'd burn it all.
Facing the wrath of giants.
Jumping straight into the fire. Trust
in my words because they are the
catalyst. I'm running headfirst into
death, and you are my witness.
Everything is for you.

Downed Lines

What useless words will I mash together to try to drive home my point? When faced with the wonder of your being, all words fail. I can feel it emanating from within you, washing me in waves like an electrical pulse. Bring me close and let me feel the static when our lips meet. For the first time, I am whole.

Makeshift Astrologer

I find myself in places I dare not tread. Focus locked on obsession and possession, their virtues shining true. Far too complex to comprehend, but I know what is right. A shaman reading bones and carving out destiny. The stars dictating the madness of our lives.

<u>Surgical Marathon</u>

To exist is to know pain. I know because I feel it every day, as feet become miles and they compound and multiply until I can no longer see the end. We weep for our own deaths, as we put faith into unknowns and words that have been said. Lay me on the table and make your incisions. Cut through to my heart and take it in your hands. It's yours to keep.

Poor Man's Christ

All I can taste is the earth in my teeth. No one knows when these wounds were infected, or the process for them to be cleaned. A razor wire halo fitted to my head. Self inflicted stigmata. Give me a martyr's death, so that I may continue to live in your heart.

Cannibal

The coils constrict my throat and
limbs, cutting my airway and
paralyzing movement. Snapping
the spine. Keeping the teeth in
straight lines, narrow and precise.
Swallowed whole. I am both the
man and the snake. Devour myself
to fuel my growth.

Self Inflicted

The shape of your face silhouetted against fire. The bone and sinew of your hand around my throat. I pray for the day we can turn off these words and just give up. Give in. Until then, we wait. Clenching our teeth and wringing our hands, cutting at our desire with the dullest of blades.

Luke on Hoth

Split me open and watch me rot. These are but shadows, poor renditions of everything I long for. Sleep in my rib cage. We've both grown tired of monotony, and can't pry the razor wire from our bellies. I will rescue you, and I will wear your skin.

Nightmare 1, the Good One

I'm running in slow motion like nightmares. Staring into mirrors. Fighting phantom figures. The deathblow from a hammer when they're crawling for the exit. This is not what it seems, because it is so much more. It's a bird of prey in flight. It's a tiger stalking prey. It's the ground splitting open and cities being swallowed into darkness. The end of the world is only the beginning.

Imaginary Trauma

In the end, there is only you. All rain and rolling clouds, boisterous thunder from the heavens. Something is beneath the soil. Something seething, begging to be exhumed. It could be death, or it could be nothing. The dirt beneath your fingernails smells of cheap wine and betrayal.

Bastard Sword

I'm bleeding out on the floor and no one can save me. These cuts are deep. From blades forged of the lives I've destroyed. I'm a Bastard. I'm a villain. Never put your trust in me, because I will betray it. Soul like tar with a crown of shattered promises, I will leech your will to carry on.

Dryad

Buried in graveyards forgotten by time. The scent of moss and rot permeates the air and brings back familiar memories of childhood in the forest. Of my older years in abandoned apartments. Both are comfort in trying times. The earthen spirits of elder gods have created the pale white skin and velvet eyes that pin me to the ground and eviscerate me in reverence to her majesty.

I Would be a Towering Inferno

Skies burning orange light the forest at twilight. I am plagued by something nameless. Swallowed whole by collapsing ground, I am nestled in the earth's womb. I am reborn, your hand pulls me free and I become as ancient gods, unholy terror. Raze the land for the queen of darkness. Give to her the sacrificial lamb. Spill the blood of children until the chalice is filled and the mothers weep into dirty palms.

There's Flies on the Wall Because of the Corpse

A single nod to a setting sun is my only goodbye. Holding onto you is gripping daggers by the blade, and I'm starting to slip. Bring me to your bedroom. Tell me I'm everything. Let me paint the walls red and give yourself to me. The adrenaline rush of holy communion in the darkness of your room.

Night Time in the City

I'm searching in darkness for any sense of comfort, and her velvet skin comes into reach. A wave of calm comes over me, like death, like the warmth of a tomb. Self medicated and drunk on the smell of perfume and summer heat.

From Nothing, Into Nothing

Do not weep, for I never existed to begin with. I was once a child, and once a young man, but became a simulacrum when I abandoned the skies in favor of earth. Driven to the ground like the loser in a dogfight. Stifle your tears, I never existed.

Emotional Vampire

The longer I speak, the more blood you lose. As if you have a choice. Vampires don't fucking sparkle. A monster is a monster and I'm no different. Guard your neck and guard your innocence, I've descended from the trees dripping spinal fluid and the sweetest whispers.

Nocturnal Son of a Bitch

We will never again see daylight, and this is constant elation. In the dark and of the dark with crooked souls to match. There is no salvation for bastards, no silver lining for monstrous anomalies. Pluck the last rose and grind it beneath your feet.

Human Waste

We're through the looking glass.
Ripped apart by jackals, and left to
the vultures, we're just carrion. A
dead prostitute in the alley. A prom
night abortion. We're all vile and
barely conscious, drifting like
ghosts through ancient cities.

Solo Riot

It's never okay when you're gone, it's all chaos and arson. Screaming and burnt flesh. Tell me it'll be okay. Tell me you admire my self destruction and the death in its wake. Pick me up from the floor and wipe off the dirt and blood. Lock me in a cage so I will sing only to you.

Hangman

Strung from lifeless trees like marionettes. All splintered wood and fraying threads, dancing in the wind with the nooses round our necks. Blossoms of razor wire. The slow motion car wreck that never ends. To have never existed would be the purest bliss.

Love is a Car Crash

I'm dragging bodies from burning wreckage again, tearing my knuckles on metal and asphalt. All lipstick and gnashing teeth. Lie with the corpses and wait for paramedics. No help is coming on these dark winding roads.

I've Seen Lord of the Rings Many, Many Times

Their roots run deep. Scattered against the backdrop of innocence; slut in a wise man's robes. When you see my eyes, you are gazing into nothingness. When we touch, I will infect you with decay. Under the shade of willows, romance is spelled out with daggers.

Like an Onion, or a Cake

A better life through vivisection. Exposing one layer at a time, laying out blood vessels. I'm not good at being human. I'm just a doppelgänger walking amongst the crowds, trying desperately not to be discovered.

Shameful Tailor

Anxiety is worn thread, hanging from my seams. Pull the string and unravel me on the floor. When I've been dissected, you will find I'm still a monster, only now I've been caged and cornered. I'm still a monster, twisted like filigree drawn in blood. Master of none and destroyer of all.

Yellow Brick Road

We became spirits when our time was erased. When it was stripped from us and fed to the lions. An eternity burning in a spiral like a halo, like the dreams we once shared. No one must know the way the cyclone has swallowed us and thrown us into other lands, forever trapped beyond the rainbow.

Base Jumper

Alone. Hollowed out and soulless.
If the devil is in the details, then I'm
the fine print. The Hieronymus
Bosch of heartbreak. The tired
cliche and poor metaphor as irony.
The man that only wants to be
whole. Throw me from the cliffs
and watch my tattered body break
on the rocks below.

Ghoul

I've been digging graves. Dirt beneath my nails and sweat upon my face. Don't mention my name. Just pretend I don't exist and that I have been erased. I've fallen into something deeper than I can escape. I'm rotting on the vine and leaving poison in my wake. I can't save face, because my face is old and weathered and it needs to be replaced. Someone give me some form of saving grace. Remove me from this place.

Atheist Beachcomber

God doesn't exist here. He abandoned us long ago, leaving us in filth. Dark tides wash away all I've built on these shores. Grains of sand like ash of burning conquest. Turn away, for your eyes are knives and I cannot bear your gaze.

Turn Me On, Dead Man

All that glimmers isn't gold, like the shimmer in my eyelids of my synapses firing; dying neurons in endless seas of black. We've played this game backwards and now we've lost it all. Locked in towers staring over vast hellscapes, the limitless power of my own foolishness.

Bipolar Tornado

They've breached the walls and now no one is safe. Hide the children. Fix the chairs beneath the doorknobs and nail the windows down. Paint the doorway with blood of the lamb and pray for morning. You may think it's the wrath of god, but it's just another mood swing.

The Inner Workings of Silence

And so it ends. We've closed the doors to the sanctum and broken keys in the locks. The grounds we tread will welcome footsteps no more, and our void shall be filled with only dust. Rejoice in sorrow, for the makers blessed us with a moment in their kingdom.

Wearing my Albatross

The ships have left the shore,
turning black against the horizon.
The fruitless search for better days.
The endless swell of the ocean.
Carry me to my tomb, cascading
pearls and mourning ghosts
swaying in the currents. The way
her fingers danced against my arm,
making my hair stand on end.

The Morning Star

Tell me it's okay. Tell me the sun has not set on you and I. To walk on sacred paths, we feign as angels for passage. Paper wings, plastic halos. I abandoned Eden only to find the world cold and unforgiving. Let me walk once more beyond heaven's gates.

Odyssey 2021

I hear the siren's call, and I will crash my vessel on the rocks. It's out of my control. It's in the hands of the gods now. Oh, cruel existence, you mock me. My body is broken, my spirit lost. Give me strength of will, for all paths lead to pain and loss.

Last Stand at Helm's Deep

The last bastion of sanity, under siege by darkness. I am the uneasy silence at a funeral. Naked and basking in flame. I am the addict shaking in his bed. Don't mourn, for the unholy fiend lies in wait on shadowed paths. Oh sweet poetry, you've only lied to me.

The First Rule

My spirit, broken and fragmented across the asphalt. Unlit roads are dangerous. They pose risks we dare not take, and enter unknowns into equations. Gentle murder behind the wheel. Headlights in my eyes. Bracing for impact as we are loved into nothingness.

Evisceration Schematic

I've drawn up schematics to destroy me. When blood no longer runs red, but rather black to match my heart, eviscerate me in the temple. Fill the carved patterns on the altar, and usher in darkness. I am evil old as man, set out like a plague to punish both the righteous and the wicked, and leave fertile lands barren.

Philip Nolan

No one can know the breadth of my sorrow. As vast and deep as oceans, the expanse of the skies. I wither on the vine. A man with no country. Homeless and abandoned by god. The eternal search for belonging, neither hindered nor completed. Steal the air from my lungs and lay me to sleep.

Death Star Trash Compactor

There exist words in the spaces between words, and I live in that poetry of twilight. The seamless fissure that crumbles the foundation. The young mare broken in the meadow. We are transients, oblivious to the wreckage in our wake.

Dance Rehearsal for Tonight's Show

Beyond pale midnights lie the cries of angels in torment. A mouth that speaks only lies. The grasp of ten tiny fingers. We exist in purgatory, devoid of joy and filled with pleasures just beyond our reach. The third trumpet sounds and Wormwood poisons the waters. We are left the most bitter taste, and the unquenched thirst of solitude.

A Beggar's Plea

Please don't cry. Your tears only cause the angels to weep. I would tear the stars from the heavens to make you smile, for only your smile can rival the glory of creation. I would take your pain if I could. Sweet woman, rest your head on my shoulder and sink into me. Let me become the panacea that forever banishes sorrow. Let me worship at the altar of your grace.

Doom Engine

What have you done? Simple fool, you have breached the gates of hell. You have tempted fate and you bring yourself only anguish. All roads lead to broken hope. Your heart is wreathed in flame, and driven through with rough hewn blades. Architect of your own sorrow.

Bacchanal

Left to the shadows that reared the ghosts that haunt me. The idiot, the laughingstock, the drunk in the gutter. I've seen this place before, and it made me feel like a fool. Well here I am again, with razors whispering my name, and the whispers all around me trying to pinpoint my shame. Trying to touch gently at the orgy. To make love with dead eyes.

Black in Technicolor

I've never seen such a radiant black. It's in my veins, and pumping through my heart. The anatomy of a partial birth abortion. The skies parting and swallowing me whole. There was a time I believed there was a future. There was a time I felt like a man.

My Own Little Floating Clod of Dirt

From here I can see the curve of the earth, and the glow of the sun against the horizon, enveloping the world in flames. We are the Nephilim, crushing man beneath our heels. Bastards cursed as neither mortal nor divine. Forever wandering, alone and detached from the place we exist.

Commodore Barry

This silence is breaking me. We stand at measured distance, yet between us endless space. I know his hands are wandering in places they don't belong, and tonight I won't sleep. You are the very air I breathe. My lungs are empty in your absence. Lay me upon that tomb once again, and allow our lips to meet as hands that pray.

And the Oscar Goes to

These are thinly veiled gestures, and I make them for your benefit. For the years have not been kind, and I am growing tired of repeating this mantra. It's dogma. It's the broken wing on a songbird. The drone of helicopters. Vast oceans cascading on foreign shores, like pornography mistaken for love.

First in Flight

There are no paths that don't end
in sadness. I am the oath breaker; I
am the grim reaper. This is me,
standing by the cliff side. Dramatic;
existential. The wings I have made
are sinew and leather, and will
catch the wind so I may soar. Or
maybe they'll shred to ribbons, and
you will find me on the forest floor.
There are no paths that make
happy endings. Hearts will break
and tears will flow like wine.

Dirty Old Men Telling Lies

Another night in the gardens of perdition, morose among blossoms of razor wire. Cold silence is my only friend. The dance of fingers on flesh. The old man's silver tongue and poison grasp. What shall it take to break the spells of ancient myths? What courage to drive the blade through the heart? Alone, in the gardens of perdition, I plot rescue and vengeance. To reclaim the throne and banish the heretic. To color silver tongues blood red. To sever digits from hands, and hands from wrists.

The Count of Monte Cristo

My heart shatters like crystal. Did you think it would be like this? Is it what you imagined? We fumble in the dark through the prisons we've built to separate us, only to find ourselves whispering through the grates in the walls. You know he'll never love you like I will. You know when fate spelled your name, she wrote it in my blood. I'll remain broken hearted until we see the folly of our ways.

Iron Lung

Conduct the symphony with the rhythm of your labored breathing. The violins bend notes that pull at the soul, were it not for the apathy that consumes me. I'm a Bastard. A psychopath out for a night on the town. Fret not, for I will be punished for my transgressions.

Unnecessary Sacrifice

You know what they say about love and distance. With the passage of time, we could become martyrs. We'll sacrifice ourselves for the benefit of others, so we can lay upon the altar just out of arms reach. Under moonlight. By the river. I pray we die with each other. The winds carry voices through the trees, begging us to follow instinct.

Death Procession

I submit. Once, this was the complex fiction of a man with little meaning. Now I am defeated. We're only leading calves to slaughter, and drinking of the blood. Covered with her death shroud, pristine alabaster. Crown of withered roses. The death rattle on the eve of my salvation.

Lovecraftian Union

A single caress is too much, but a thousand days enveloped by you will never be enough. As the sword pierces flesh, so your eyes peer through my heart. Like ancient gods who stir in deep ocean trenches, bringing madness to the world, our separation spells the end of pleasure and comfort. Without you, only sadness. Without you, nothing more.

Mausoleum Tour

Sanguine, stained; the frailty of these hands could not hold what once was pure and just. A pallid funeral shroud like being wed in beautiful decay, and the sweetest scent hanging amidst stagnant air. I am tragedy's companion. An unkindness of ravens the requiem for the innocence lost, and the way all good men become devils.

Electrical Buckshot

The ambient drone of power lines, the soundtrack to oblivion. Like a tidal wave to wash away my iniquities. A shotgun to the abdomen. Nothing matters in the face of this loss.

Father Mother

My virtue passed with 10,000 sunsets. The whore as mother figure. The soulless preacher's sermon. Exhausting all options to mask my sadness.

Prey and Predator

If these lips could only utter one
word, it would be your name.
Beneath the vulture's wing, losing
bits of me; akin to the dismantling
of sanity when you are away.
Disconnected. Mend the break and
place me in your arms. The
saccharine whispers from the
mouth of a tiger, like sedated
lullabies ushering in sleep.

Graveyard Holiday

We walk among the corpses and shudder at daylight. The last blossoms of spring have loosened their petals, and just like them, I die in the summer. A wound to the side, the spear of Longinus, the fatted calf. The weathered fabric in the branches shivers in the wind. I'm alone in the fallout.

Devil's Throat

There exists only heartache. My footsteps shall never haunt these sacred halls. As kingdoms rise and fall, I remain shackled to this throne of woe. Exiled from eden, to the mouth of Tartarus. We only pass as do strangers, walking along the precipice of blissful obsolescence.

The End

The politics of loss. Adrift in nameless seas, pleading for you to consider me. I want to be more than just warmth and safety. I want to be more than everything. Take down your hair and fall into me. We are but bodies, doing what bodies should do. Don't deny this is right. The emptiness of this room and of my heart are only ripples in the wake of your absence.

Tim Pangburn is a professional artist who works in many mediums from writing, to tattooing, to mixed media assemblage. He lives in Bucks County, Pennsylvania with his wife and two sons, and (sometimes) three daughters. You can follow his blog at www.timpangburn.com, and his art on Instagram @timpangburnomg. You can contact him via email at timothypangburn@gmail.com.

Made in the USA
Middletown, DE
13 October 2021

49986011R00059